EDGE BOOKS

The American Revolution

BY THE NUMBERS

by Amanda Lanser

Consultant:

Robert J. Allison PhD

Chair, History

Suffolk University

Boston, Massachusetts

CAPSTONE PRESS
a capstone imprint

Edge Books are published by Capstone Press,
1710 Roe Crest Drive, North Mankato, Minnesota 56003
www.capstonepub.com

Library of Congress Cataloging-in-Publication Data
Lanser, Amanda.
 The American Revolution by the numbers / by Amanda Lanser.
    pages cm.—(Edge books. America at war by the numbers.)
 Summary: "Describes aspects of the American Revolution using numbers,
stats, and infographics"—Provided by publisher.
 Includes bibliographical references and index.
 ISBN 978-1-4914-4294-4 (library binding)
 ISBN 978-1-4914-4330-9 (eBook PDF)
 1. United States—History—Revolution, 1775–1783—Juvenile literature.
 I. Title.
 E208.L28 2016
 973.3—dc23   2015000534

Editorial Credits
Arnold Ringstad, editor
Craig Hinton, designer and production specialist

Photo Credits
AP Images: Corbis/Bettmann, cover (all), 1; Corbis: Bettmann, 10; Library of Congress: Prints and Photographs Division, 5, 11 (top),
29 (bottom), Benjamin Franklin, 7 (bottom background), Edward P. Moran, 26; National Archives and Records Administration: 2 (top),
14–15; North Wind Picture Archives, 4, 8, 9 (all), 17 (middle, bottom), 20–21 (all), 27; Shutterstock: American Spirit, 7 (silhouette),
Andrew F. Kazmierski, 6 (silhouette), David Smart, 3 (left), 7 (top), Melinda Fawyer, 23 (top), Nicholas Rjabow, 23 (bottom),
wavebreakmedia, 3 (right), 6 (background); U.S. National Guard: Domenick D'Andrea, 22; U.S. Navy, 11 (bottom), 13; Wikimedia:
Charles Wilson Peale, 16, Emanuel Leutze, 24–25, Howard Pyle, 12, John Trumbull, 28–29, Richard Purcell, 17 (top)

Design Element
Red Line Editorial (infographics); Shutterstock Images: Ken Schulze (smoke)

Printed in the United States of America in North Mankato, Minnesota.
122015   009362R

Table of Contents

The anger of the American colonists was rising. By the 1700s Great Britain owned several colonies in North America. Britain's **Parliament** passed laws applying heavy taxes to the colonists, including the Stamp Act in 1765. Yet there was no representation for American interests in Parliament. The cry of the colonists became, "No taxation without representation." This is the struggle for the colonists' independence—the American Revolution—by the numbers.

Setting the Stage for War

0 members of the British Parliament who represented the American colonists

2.5 million estimated population of American colonies in 1775

6.4 million estimated population of Great Britain by 1770

£100,000 estimated amount of money to be received each year from American colonists as a result of the Stamp Act

£60,000 approximate cost of a large British warship in the 1760s

THE FOLLY OF ENGLAND AND THE RUIN OF AMERICA

colonist—a person who settles in a new territory that is governed by his or her home country
Parliament—the legislature of Great Britain

4

Anger in Boston

The colonists' anger grew after March 5, 1770. On that day a crowd gathered in Boston, Massachusetts, to protest the presence of British troops there. Some of the troops fired into the crowd.

8
British soldiers involved in the Boston Massacre

400
estimated number of Americans in the angry crowd

0 British soldiers killed

5 American colonists killed by British soldiers

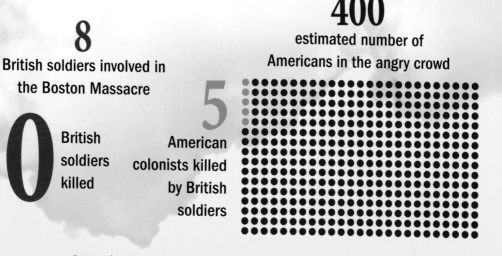

American anger erupted again in December 1773. Frustrated colonists boarded a British ship in Boston Harbor and dumped its cargo of tea into the water to protest tea taxes. The event became known as the Boston Tea Party.

92,000 pounds of tea dumped during the Boston Tea Party

342 chests of tea the colonists dumped overboard

4 number of new laws the British put into place after the Boston Tea Party to punish the colonists. The laws became known as the

£9,659 value of the dumped tea in 1773. That translates to $1.7 million today.

Loyalists and Patriots

Tensions were boiling over in the American colonies by the spring of 1775. Some colonists wished to remain British citizens. These people were known as loyalists. Those who favored independence were called patriots. Others were neutral on the issue. The slogan "Join, or Die" was printed in newspapers, encouraging the colonists to band together against the British.

19,000

loyalists who served in the British army

100,000

loyalists who left the country after the American Revolution ended

231,771

enlisted patriots who had served in the Continental army by the end of the war in 1783

164,087

patriots who had served in state **militias** by the end of the war in 1783

50%
colonists who strongly supported the patriot cause

30%
colonists who were neutral

20%
colonists who strongly supported the loyalist cause

The Battles of Lexington and Concord

Parliament declared Massachusetts to be in **rebellion** in February 1775. The British sent 700 troops toward the town of Concord on April 14 to destroy weapons stored there. Colonial militias met some of the troops in Lexington before they could reach Concord. The clashes that followed were the first battles of the American Revolution. The militias forced the British to retreat to Boston.

70 militiamen who met the troops on Lexington Green

8 militiamen who died at Lexington Green

0 British soldiers who died at Lexington Green

15,000 militiamen who surrounded Boston, trapping the British in the city

400 men in the **"minutemen"** militia who met British troops on the North Bridge in Concord

2,000 approximate number of militia troops who attacked the British as they retreated from Concord to Boston

April 18, 1775

the date of Paul Revere's famous ride

Paul Revere was an American silversmith deeply involved in the patriot cause. Before the war, he had participated in the Boston Tea Party. Later, in April 1775, he helped signal the British departure from Boston to Concord by placing lanterns in a high tower in Boston. He then rode his horse across the countryside from Boston to Lexington to warn fellow patriots that the British were approaching. The warning he provided made it possible for minutemen to prepare for the battle at Lexington before the British reached Concord.

2 lanterns to be placed in the tower if the British were approaching by water on the Charles River

1 lantern to be placed in the tower if the British were approaching by land

Continental Forces

Continental Army and Militias

250,000

200,000

150,000

100,000

50,000

0

Continental Army

State Militias

total number of men enlisted

231,771 men enlisted in the Continental army between 1775 and 1783

20,000 men in the Continental army at any one point in time

1–3 average years of service for a Continental army soldier

164,087 men serving in state militias between 1775 and 1783

16 minimum age for serving in a state militia

1 minute time it took soldiers in special groups in Massachusetts to ready themselves for battle, leading to the nickname "minutemen"

Continental Army Soldiers

20–25 average age of Continental army soldiers in 1777

1 pound of beef or ¾ pound of pork allowed to each soldier per day

2 swords owned by officers; one was for ceremonies and the other was for battle

Continental Navy

7 number of ships in the Continental navy's first fleet

$125 money earned per month in Continental dollars by the Continental navy's first commander, Esek Hopkins

200 approximate number of British ships captured by the Continental navy during the war

British
Forces

British Army

50,000
British troops who fought
in the Revolutionary War

200
soldiers in each group of British
infantry known as a regiment

3
years of service that made
soldiers eligible for **discharge**
after the war ended

5–15
average years of experience of
ordinary British soldiers

infantry—soldiers who fight on foot
discharge—to be released from military duty

British Navy

Number of ships from 1776 to 1783

500

270

500	
400	
300	
200	

1776

1783

74 typical number of cannons on Royal Navy ships

1 pound of biscuits British sailors received daily

1st rank of the British in worldwide naval power in 1776

Boston and Bunker Hill

Two months after the Battles of Lexington and Concord, American militiamen were still laying **siege** to Boston. State militias were stationed in the area, including some atop Bunker Hill in Charlestown, overlooking Boston. British generals decided to remove the militias. The British were able to take Bunker Hill eventually, but they suffered heavy **casualties**. Although they lost the hill, the Americans had proved their commitment to independence. The siege eventually ended after George Washington used captured artillery to force the British to leave the city.

11 months

length of the siege of Boston (April 19, 1775–March 17, 1776)

6,500 British soldiers trapped in Boston

50 approximate number of cannons Washington aimed at Boston to force the British to evacuate

siege—the act of surrounding a city and its inhabitants in hopes of forcing a surrender

casualty—a soldier who is dead, wounded, missing, or captured after a battle

160 feet length of the earthen fort the Americans made atop Bunker Hill

30 feet height of the earthen fort

24 hours time it took the Americans to fortify Bunker Hill

1 day the Battle of Bunker Hill lasted (June 17, 1775)

3 waves of attacks the British made against the Americans on Bunker Hill

1,000 American militiamen who fought in the Battle of Bunker Hill

2,400 British soldiers who fought in the Battle of Bunker Hill

American Casualties

34%

66%

British Casualties

21%

79%

■ dead
■ wounded

140 dead, 271 wounded

226 dead, 828 wounded

Commander-in-Chief Major General
George Washington

June 15, 1775–December 23, 1783: time Washington served as the general and **commander-in-chief** of the Continental army

0 number of armies Washington commanded before the Continental army

9 number of Revolutionary War battles fought

3 number of Revolutionary War battles won

Battle Timeline

■ American victory   ■ British victory   ■ Draw

	Battle of Bunker Hill 6/17/1775	Siege of Boston 4/1775–3/1776	Battle of Long Island 8/27/1776	Battle of Trenton 12/26/1776	Battle of Princeton 1/3/1777
Washington		✕	✕	✕	✕
Howe	✕	✕	✕		
Clinton		✕	✕		
Cornwallis			✕		✕

commander-in-chief—the military officer in command of a country's military

Commander-in-Chief General 🇬🇧 William Howe

1775–1778:
time Howe served as commander-in-chief of the British army in North America

7 years of prior military leadership experience in the French and Indian War (1754–1763)

1778–1781:
time Clinton served as commander-in-chief of the British army in North America

6 years of prior military leadership experience in the British army

General 🇬🇧 Henry Clinton

🇬🇧 General Charles Cornwallis

1776–1781:
time Cornwallis served as a major general of the British army in North America

16 years of prior military leadership experience in the British army

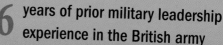

	Battle of Brandywine 9/11/1777	Battle of Germantown 10/4/1777	Battle of Monmouth 6/28/1778	Siege of Charleston 3/29/1780– 5/12/1780	Siege of Yorktown 9/28/1781– 10/19/1781
	✖	✖	✖		✖
	✖	✖			
			✖	✖	
	✖	✖	✖	✖	✖

Foreign Influence

Great Britain

13 Colonies and Allies

North America

American Allies

3 countries that aided the American cause (France, Spain, and the Netherlands)

The Iroquois Confederacy

1777 year the Iroquois Confederacy decided to participate in the war

6 American Indian Nations in the Iroquois Confederacy in 1777

American Indian Nation	British Allies	American Allies
Cayuga	✗	
Mohawk	✗	
Oneida		✗
Onondaga	✗	
Seneca	✗	
Tuscarora		✗

11,000

muskets the French supplied to the Americans by 1777

6,000

French soldiers who arrived in America in July 1780

1,000

barrels of gunpowder the French supplied to the Americans by 1777

$1.4 billion

value, in today's dollars, of supplies and weapons the French gave to the Americans

Europe

British Allies

30,000

German **mercenaries** hired to fight alongside the British

1779 year Spain joined

1 number of territories Spain regained from the British by supporting the Americans (Florida)

musket—a type of gun with a long barrel used in the 1700s
mercenary—a soldier hired to fight for another country's army

Revolutionary Spies

Nathan Hale was an important spy for the Continental army during the early years of the war. He joined the military in Connecticut in 1775. He then traveled to New York and volunteered for a spying mission against the British. Caught in late 1776, he was executed by the British. Hale is remembered as a hero in the American Revolution.

1 number of spying missions Hale carried out

September 21, 1776 date Nathan Hale was captured by the British while trying to escape British-held territory

21 Hale's age at the time of his execution

September 21, 1780

date that Continental army General Benedict Arnold met with British military spy John André, providing him with information about the Continental army. André was caught and executed in October. Arnold escaped to Great Britain.

£20,000

the amount of money Arnold requested from the British in exchange for his betrayal

The Culper Spy Ring worked to provide George Washington with information on the location and movement of British troops. The identities of the spies were kept secret. Even Washington did not know who the spies supplying him with information were.

763

number of code numbers used to identify spies and other sensitive information

711

code number for George Washington

745

code number for Britain

727

code number for New York

16

age of Sybil Ludington, who rode across the Connecticut countryside in secret in 1777 to warn nearby militiamen that British troops were approaching

5

years the Culper Spy Ring was in operation

Revolutionary
Weapons

20–30 rounds of ammunition each Continental army soldier carried

3–4 shots a musket could fire per minute

48.7 inches length of a Revolutionary War-era musket

100 yards range of a musket

1,400 yards

maximum range
of mortars

13 inches

maximum **caliber**
of mortars

45 degrees

angle at which
mortars were fired

2,000 yards

maximum range of field cannons

3 and 6 pounds

weight of common
cannon balls

range—the maximum distance a weapon can accurately fire
caliber—the width of a weapon's barrel

Crossing the Delaware
and the Battle of Trenton

General Washington led his men across the Delaware River on December 25, 1776. They launched a surprise attack on the German soldiers fighting for the British in Trenton, New Jersey. Thick snow made the crossing and the march to Trenton difficult. However, the attack was a success. Washington's men captured enemy soldiers and supplies.

2,400 soldiers who crossed the Delaware River with Washington

10 miles distance from the camp on the Delaware River to Trenton, New Jersey

1 mile length of the troop and supply train on the road to Trenton

Leutze's Painting

Emanuel Leutze's famous painting, *Washington Crossing the Delaware*, is an iconic image in American history. However, some things in the image were changed or added for dramatic effect.

60 feet length of the actual boats used in the crossing, which were flat ferries rather than rowboats

300 yards width of the river at the actual area where the crossing happened, much narrower than shown in the painting

1777 year that the flag shown in the painting was actually adopted, one year after the events in the painting

Estimated number of German soldiers at Trenton **1,400**

900 Estimated number of German soldiers captured by American troops in the Battle of Trenton

| 0 | 300 | 600 | 900 | 1,200 | 1,500 |

1 hours the surprise attack lasted

2 days Washington's troops marched and fought in rain, snow, sleet, and hail

Valley Forge and the Battle of Monmouth

The Continental army suffered multiple losses in late 1777. Washington led the army to set up camp at Valley Forge, Pennsylvania. There they would wait out a challenging winter. Severe cold, a lack of food, and disease killed thousands. But the disciplined troops regrouped. They captured nearby Philadelphia in June 1778.

2,000
men who died from diseases such as typhoid and smallpox at Valley Forge in the winter of 1777–1778

12,000
soldiers stationed at Valley Forge in December 1777

2
men whose executions Washington canceled after being overjoyed at the news the French had joined the war against the British. The men had been charged with desertion for leaving the military without permission.

5
months that Prussian-born American general Friedrich von Steuben trained the Continental army at Valley Forge

Washington led the Continental army against British troops retreating from Philadelphia through New Jersey on June 28. The clash was called the Battle of Monmouth. The Americans attacked the rear of the marching British forces. The attack spurred the British to continue their march through the night, rather than rest until morning. Neither side won a clear victory.

12 miles
length of the British supply train

18,000
British and German troops who retreated from Philadelphia

200 American casualties

6,000
American soldiers who attacked the rear of the retreating British forces

358
British casualties, including those who died of heatstroke

The Yorktown Campaign
and the
Treaty of Paris

The Continental army and the French surrounded British troops in the city of Yorktown, Virginia, on September 29, 1781. The British finally surrendered on October 19. The surrender ended the six years of fighting that had begun at Lexington and Concord in 1775. The Treaty of Paris officially declared the United States to be independent from Britain.

7,000 number of British troops Cornwallis surrendered

10 days between the Americans' attack on Yorktown and General Cornwallis' surrender

41 number of artillery guns that opened fire on Yorktown on October 9

20 days of the siege of Yorktown

684 days between the British surrender at Yorktown and the signing of the Treaty of Paris

treaty—a formal agreement between two or more nations
ratify—to approve in an official way

Treaty of Paris: One, Two, Three

1 British negotiator involved in drafting the Treaty of Paris (David Hartley)

2 crucial ideas the Americans required in the Treaty of Paris:

★ Britain's recognition of the United States as an independent nation

★ creation of boundaries in North America that would allow the United States to expand westward

3 American negotiators involved in drafting the Treaty of Paris (John Adams, Benjamin Franklin, and John Jay)

January 14, 1784

date American representatives **ratified** the Treaty of Paris

GLOSSARY

caliber (CAL-uh-bur)—the width of a weapon's barrel

casualty (KAZH-yul-tee)—a soldier who is dead, wounded, missing, or captured after a battle

colonist (KOL-uh-nist)—a person who settles in a new territory that is governed by his or her home country

commander-in-chief (kuh-MAN-dur-IN-CHEEF)—the military officer in command of a country's military

discharge (dis-CHARG)—to be released from military duty

enlisted (en-LIST-ed)—enrolled in the army or other branch of the military

infantry (IN-fuhn-tree)—soldiers who fight on foot

mercenary (MUR-se-nair-ee)—a soldier hired to fight for another country's army

militia (muh-LISH-uh)—a group of citizens who may be called to military duty

minuteman (MIN-it-man)—a young militiaman who was specially trained to respond quickly in military emergencies

musket (MUHSS-kit)—a type of gun with a long barrel used in the 1700s

Parliament (PAR-luh-ment)—the legislature of Great Britain

range (RAYNJ)—the maximum distance a weapon can accurately fire

ratify (RAT-uh-fye)—to approve in an official way

rebellion (ree-BEL-yun)—a fight against one's own government or other authority

siege (SEEJ)—the act of surrounding a city and its inhabitants in hopes of forcing a surrender

treaty (TREE-tee)—a formal agreement between two or more nations

READ MORE

Burgan, Michael. *The Split History of the American Revolution: A Perspectives Flip Book*. Perspectives Flip Books. North Mankato, Minn.: Compass Point Books, 2013.

Forest, Christopher. *The Biggest Battles of the Revolutionary War*. The Story of the American Revolution. North Mankato, Minn.: Capstone Press, 2013.

Grayson, Robert. *Revolutionary War*. Essential Library of American Wars. Minneapolis, Minn.: ABDO Publishing Company, 2014.

CRITICAL THINKING USING THE COMMON CORE

1. Look at pages 16 and 17. The military leaders of the Revolutionary War entered the conflict with different amounts of experience. In what ways do you think the experience helped the British? What advantages did the Continental army have that could have helped make up for its lack of experienced soldiers? (Key Ideas and Details)

2. What do pages 10 and 11 tell you about the soldiers who fought for independence during the American Revolution? How did they compare to British forces? Support your answer with at least two other online or print sources. (Integration of Knowledge and Ideas)

INTERNET SITES

FactHound offers a safe, fun way to find Internet sites related to this book. All of the sites on FactHound have been researched by our staff.

Visit *www.facthound.com*

Type in this code: 9781491442944

INDEX

TITLES IN THIS SET:

The American
Revolution
BY THE NUMBERS

THE
CIVIL WAR
BY THE NUMBERS

WORLD
WAR I
BY THE NUMBERS

WORLD
WAR II
BY THE NUMBERS